Memories and Life Lessons

from the

MAGIC TREE HOUSE®

Memories and Life Lessons

from the

MAGIC TREE HOUSE®

MARY POPE OSBORNE

with illustrations by Sal Murdocca

RANDOM HOUSE 🏠 NEW YORK

All rights reserved. Published in the United States by Random House Children's Books, a division of Penguin Random House LLC, New York. The illustrations that appear herein were originally published in different form in various Magic Tree House titles.

Random House and the colophon are registered trademarks of Penguin Random House LLC.

Magic Tree House is a registered trademark of Mary Pope Osborne; used under license.

Photograph credits: Courtesy of Mary Pope Osborne (pp. 124–129); copyright © Bill Pope (pp. 130–131); copyright © Will Osborne (p. 132).

Visit us on the Web! rhcbooks.com

Educators and librarians, for a variety of teaching tools, visit us at RHTeachersLibrarians.com

Library of Congress Cataloging-in-Publication Data is available upon request.
ISBN 978-0-593-48454-8 (trade) — ISBN 978-0-593-48460-9 (lib. bdg.) — ISBN 978-0-593-48455-5 (ebook)

The text of this book is set in 12-point Century Expanded BT.
Interior design by Danielle Deschenes and Elizabeth Tardiff

MANUFACTURED IN CHINA
10 9 8 7 6 5 4 3 2 1
First Edition

To Michael, Bill, and Natalie
And to the memory of our parents

CONTENTS

Dear Reader,

After nearly thirty years of seeing the world through the eyes of Jack and Annie, I decided to collect some of the insights they'd gained into a single book. As I began to gather "life lessons" from more than sixty Magic Tree House adventures, I found myself connecting those lessons to experiences in my own childhood.

As memories surfaced, I was surprised to realize how many seeds of the tree house stories were planted long ago in my early life. I laughed at how peculiar I was as a child, and how my runaway imagination seemed to keep me about two feet off the ground at all times. Mostly, I was grateful for how much my family helped me feel safe, in spite of my inordinate number of childhood fears.

I hope readers, young and old alike, will find pieces of themselves in my memories—as well as feel fortified by Jack and Annie's hard-earned wisdom and dauntless courage. I've always wished I were more like the two of them. Writing the books has given me the illusion that I am.

Mary Pope Osborne

BE GLAD TO BE ALIVE

1

Jack grabbed one of his books about ancient Rome. He looked in the index and found *Marcus Aurelius.*

He found the right page and read . . . a quote from Marcus Aurelius:

"When you arise in the morning, think of what a precious privilege it is to be alive, to think, to enjoy, to love. . . ."

"No problem," whispered Jack.

—Warriors in Winter

W hen I was six and seven years old, the children in my family had remarkable freedom. We lived in Fort Monroe, Virginia, one of the oldest army posts in the U.S. Our living area was surrounded by a moat with two tunnels that connected us to the rest of the post. In the middle of our area was a parade field bordered by spreading trees, houses built in the 1800s, and a beautiful small church called the Chapel of the Centurion. We could frequently hear its bells ringing.

I loved to get up early on summer mornings with my twin brother, Bill, and our brother, Michael, who was a year and a half younger. After breakfast, our mom would release us to the outdoors as if she were freeing birds to the wind. Sometimes we'd join up with our friend Chris and walk to the PX, which was a military department store. Before the store opened, we'd pull big cardboard boxes from its dumpster. Then we'd carry them across the empty parade field in the early light and make believe the boxes were our little houses. Now and then, we'd stop and pretend to sleep in them, and then continue on our way.

*If you greet the morning
with joy and enthusiasm,
your day can be filled with
great adventures.*

"Annie, *listen*!" said Jack.

Annie stopped talking and listened to the rustling leaves of the giant trees. More and more sounds filled the evening air . . . the strange, whirring voices of all the living things of Yosemite. The wind stirred the voices together, blending them into one timeless, wordless song.

—Camp Time in California

rowing up, I was afraid of many things: spiders, ants, mosquitoes, and tidal waves, to name just a few. But I was *never* afraid of climbing trees. Trees were my gateway into the mysterious world of nature.

Our military family moved to a new house every couple of years. Wherever we landed, my brothers and I would end up in nearby trees. In Fort Monroe, we each chose our own tree. Mine was an oak tree. The boys and I thought a tree house would be a great addition to one of our trees, but we didn't know how to build one. So we made do with grabbing hold of branches and climbing until we couldn't climb any higher. I loved it when the wind started to blow and the branches swayed and leaves quaked and whispered, and anything seemed possible. I climbed trees until I was thirteen. Even today, I can't pass a tree with low, spreading branches without wanting to climb it.

———

Find your own gateway into the natural world. The rewards will last a lifetime.

"You have to go back to Father Laurent now, Barry," Jack said softly. He tugged on Barry's velvety ear. "But we think you're a *great* dog. . . . Annie, aren't you going to say good-bye to him?"

Annie knelt down and put her arms around Barry's giant head. He licked her as she clutched him.

"Tell him, Annie," Jack urged her.

Annie lifted Barry's ear and whispered into it for a long time. Jack couldn't hear all that she said, but he caught the words *love* and *all my life*.

—Dogs in the Dead of Night

*O*ne of my biggest regrets is that I was afraid of dogs as a child. I remember walking to the parade field one morning when I was seven and spotting a neighbor's huge white dog. Even though I knew this dog was friendly, I ran to a tree and climbed it. The dog just wandered around the field while I sat high on a branch, anxiously waiting for him to go back home.

Years later, I fell in love with a very old golden retriever named Teddy. He lived about half a mile from a cabin my husband, Will, and I owned in Pennsylvania. Teddy would mysteriously appear at our door whenever we visited the cabin. One winter midnight, I saw Teddy standing in the moonlit snow. I invited him inside. I dried his cold golden fur, and soon he and I fell asleep together. At dawn, I walked Teddy outside and sent him back home. For a long time afterward, I felt as if a fairy-tale prince had visited the cabin that winter night.

Teddy inspired us to get our own puppy, a small terrier we named Bailey. In my mind, Teddy will always be the leader of the dog parade that has since marched through our lives.

———

Love dogs. Start now.

DISCOVER
THE MAGIC OF BOOKS

2

The sound of a horse's whinny came from below.

Neeee-hhhh!

"I think we're here," whispered Annie. She was still holding the castle book.

Jack peeked out the window.

A huge castle loomed out of the fog.

Jack looked around. The tree house was in a different oak tree.

"Look!" said Annie.

Down below, a knight on a black horse was riding by.

"Oh, man," said Jack, "that's incredible."

—The Knight at Dawn

I remember one of the first times that the magic of reading happened to me. In first grade, I was looking at a story about a pig riding a bicycle on a sunny day. As I was figuring out the words, I imagined riding my own blue bike. I pictured riding along a dirt path near our house . . . and suddenly *I* was the pig riding a bike on a sunny day! I felt the air and the sunlight and the excitement the pig felt as he set out on his adventure. I went from there to being a large rabbit in the Uncle Wiggily books, a pioneer girl in *Little House on the Prairie,* and a Japanese boy in *The Big Wave.* Since the day I became a pig on a bicycle, I've been thousands of creatures and people, thanks to books.

———

Read a book, and be anything
you'd like to be.

"Indeed," said Morgan. "You have proved that you can find answers to very hard questions."

She reached into the folds of her robe and took out two thin pieces of wood.

"A magic library card for each of you," she said. She gave one to Annie and one to Jack.

"Oh, man," said Jack. . . .

"These are your Master Librarian cards," said Morgan. "You are the newest members of the ancient Society of Master Librarians."

—Polar Bears Past Bedtime

One of the first things our family did when we moved to a new army post was to visit the local library and get library cards. If the library wasn't too far from our house, my brothers and I would ride our bicycles there and return home with baskets filled with books. Michael read all the Tarzan books. Bill read books about the weather, World War II, and natural disasters. I read Nancy Drew books and, later, Agatha Christie and Sherlock Holmes mysteries.

When I lived in New York City, I haunted every city library I could find. I practically lived in the libraries, doing research for the Magic Tree House series. I researched the time of dinosaurs, knights and castles, ancient Egypt, pirates of the Caribbean, ninja warriors of Japan, a rain forest on the Amazon, and dozens of people and places from around the world. All the time-travel adventures I've had in libraries feel as real to me now as if I'd actually traveled to the places I studied.

———

Read a book, and have adventures around the world without ever leaving your town.

"In the night, you can see all the story characters that saved you on your last four missions," said Morgan. "They are all here— Hercules and the silk weaver; Sarph, the serpent monster; and Pegasus." . . .

"Where are they, Morgan?" cried Annie. "Where's Pegasus?"

"Look hard," said Morgan.

"I can't see him!" said Annie.

"Yes, you can," said Morgan. "The old stories are always with us. We are never alone. . . . The ancient Greeks named one of their constellations Pegasus."

She waved her hand again and the white horse's head, wings, and galloping legs glowed in the sky.

—Hour of the Olympics

W hen I was a young adult, at the end of a long journey, I found myself in a hospital in Nepal. I was very ill with blood poisoning, too ill even to figure out how to contact my family. I happened to have a thick book with me—the *Lord of the Rings* trilogy by J. R. R. Tolkien. For two weeks, I spent all my waking time lying in my hospital bed, reading the trilogy. The book comforted me beyond words. It gave me instant imaginary friends. Those friends were funny, brave, and kind. They helped give me the strength to figure out how to fly home to the States so I could get well.

Over the years, I've collected many different copies of *The Lord of the Rings*. When I see those books on my shelf, I always feel as if I'm among friends.

Search for friends and comfort in good books.

Have Compassion
For All Creatures

3

"Besides contemplating the universe, what else do you think about?" Aristotle asked Annie.

"Um . . . I think a lot about animals," she said.

"Wonderful. Animals always reveal to us something natural and beautiful," said Aristotle. "So you study them?"

"I *do* study them," Annie said. "But more than that, I fall in love with them. I think that's the way I really learn."

"Ah, very good," said Aristotle. "To truly educate your mind, you must also educate your heart."

—*Stallion by Starlight*

My brother Michael had a friend named Neil. Neil and Michael were both trying to earn Cub Scout badges. I would supervise their efforts and verify when I thought they'd succeeded. But that's not the main thing I remember about Neil. What I remember most is that he had a small green turtle named Chlorophyll the Eighth.

"Why 'the Eighth'?" we asked him.

Neil explained that Chlorophyll was the eighth in a long line of previous turtles he'd also named Chlorophyll. So after Chlorophyll the First, there'd been a Chlorophyll the Second, Chlorophyll the Third, and so on. It was startling to learn that so many little turtles had passed away in Neil's care. I worried a lot about Neil's latest turtle. For a while, when I said prayers at night, I added "Chlorophyll the Eighth" to my list of loved ones who might need protection.

Have compassion for your
neighbor's pets, as well
as your own.

Basho laughed. . . .

"A poet needs to live with the wind and the clouds, the flowers and the birds. Here, I have a small garden and my banana tree. I have the sound of the river all day long. Here, I have everything I need to write my poems."

"What do you write about?" asked Annie.

"Small things," said Basho. "A crow picking snails out of the mud, a woodpecker hammering a tree, pine needles scattered by the wind. A poet finds beauty in all the small things of nature."

—*Dragon of the Red Dawn*

*E*very few years, our family would drive to a rural town in Alabama to visit Mama Dickens, our mother's mother. Mama Dickens kept chickens in her backyard, and one hot early morning, when my brothers and I were five and six years old, we were stretched out on an old iron bed, watching the chickens through the screen window. We started talking to them, giving them directions, such as "Walk to the left," "Walk toward the house," "Walk to the right." Astonishingly, the chickens did exactly what we told them! It only happened that one time. But for years, the three of us felt mysteriously connected to Mama Dickens's chickens.

———

Try to connect with ordinary creatures, and discover how extraordinary they really are.

Leaves, branches, puddles, bushes, grass, vines, wild flowers—all glittered like jewels.

Or gleamed like gold.

Annie had been right, thought Jack.

Forget the treasure chest.

They had treasure at home. A ton of it. Everywhere.

—Pirates Past Noon

One afternoon, I saw two insects attached to our screen door: One was a walking stick insect, which looked *exactly* like a small twig. Coincidentally, next to the walking stick was a dead-leaf moth, which looked *exactly* like a dead leaf.

I stood at the screen door for a long time, amazed. I've never forgotten them. What if I had just walked by, thinking only of myself? Miracles can easily go unnoticed.

Look outside yourself
to find unexpected treasure
all around you.

REACH OUT TO OTHERS

4

"Our mother says friendship is like riding the waves," said Kama. "Sometimes you ride low, gentle waves. Sometimes you ride high, rough ones."

Annie gasped. She looked at Jack. She repeated Morgan's rhyme:

To find a special magic,
build a special kind of ship
that rides the waves,
both high and low,
on every kind of trip.

"*Friendship! That's the ship!*" said Jack.

—High Tide in Hawaii

*T*he summer between first and second grade, my brothers and I loved taking voyages on an old green picnic table in our yard in Fort Monroe. We pretended it was a ship that could take us all over the world. I was the cook on the ship and made pretend meals out of grass and dirt. And sometimes we snuck a bag of real cookies onboard.

When our friend Chris first moved into a house down the street, we invited him to play with us. We pulled him aboard our green picnic-table ship. I remember Chris and Michael feeding bits of a cookie through the open mouth of one of my dolls. (Later that doll had an issue with ants.) Before our first voyage with Chris ended, we were all best friends.

Invite new neighbors to come aboard, and life can become even more fun.

Annie was standing under a streetlamp,
cradling the puppy in her arms.

"Let me see him," said Jack. He parked the
bikes and looked at the puppy under the light. The
tiny dog had beautiful big brown eyes. His curly
black-and-white fur was soft and shiny.

"Ohh," said Jack, stroking the furry little head.
"He's really cute."

"Let's get him home," said Annie. "I'm sure he's
hungry and thirsty."

—*Balto of the Blue Dawn*

One warm autumn day while I was driving in the country, I noticed a small dog with curly white hair, trotting down the middle of the road. Even though he was panting in the heat, he had a jaunty, confident step. I pulled over and picked him up. He had no collar, so I carried him from house to house, searching for his owner. Finally, someone told me he belonged to a gardener working nearby. When I took him to the gardener, the first thing she said was "Do you want him?" He'd recently been rescued from a bad home, and she was his foster mother. He was about four years old and needed a permanent, loving family.

For the next thirteen years, Little Bear was my shadow. He was an inscrutable dog, who kept his thoughts and feelings to himself. But he never wanted me out of his sight. For all those years, he walked behind me through our house. No matter how deeply he slept, it was impossible to sneak away from him. If there was a closed door between us, he'd tirelessly peer under it to see where I was. Even when he was seventeen years old and blind, he tracked my every step. Now that he's gone, I still feel his presence, following gratefully behind me. He'll never let me go.

*Invite a homeless animal
to join your life. Then try to be
worthy of their gratitude.*

Jack read aloud:

Love hides in plain sight. We are never all alone.

"Whoa," said Annie. "It might sound simple. But it's deep."

"It is?" said Jack.

"Yes, Tenzin proved it," said Annie.

"How?" said Jack.

"After he lost his family, he felt all alone and just stayed in his house," said Annie. "But Morgan's note made him climb the mountain again. He found his old friend, the snow leopard. The Guardian of the Mountains. And she reminded him that she was always there, that love is all around us, protecting us. Even when we can't see it."

—Sunlight on the Snow Leopard

When I was a young adult, I lived for a while in Monterey, California. Much of the time, I was sad and lonely. Sometimes I would wander to the Old Fisherman's Wharf and walk by the boats, food carts, and street entertainers. One of the entertainers was an organ-grinder—a man who cranked a little hand organ and walked with a pet monkey who wore a red jacket and a cap. One day, walking along the wharf, I stopped near the organ-grinder. The little monkey noticed me and held out his hand for me to shake. When I felt the grasp of the monkey's tiny, warm fingers, a tenderness passed between us. And I started to cry! I thanked the monkey and quickly headed back home, sniffing and smiling at the same time. I knew I had to find some friends and reach out to my family.

If a kind monkey offers its hand,
be sure to take it. It might
help you change your life
for the better.

LOOK FOR HEROES, FAR AND NEAR

5

Jack looked at George Washington.

"Even if things look impossible, you should keep going, sir," he said. "The harder things seem, the greater the triumph, right? That's what you read to your men. You have to keep going for *their* sake."

"Yes! And you have to keep going for *our* sake," said Annie. "For the sake of the *future* children of America, sir."

—*Revolutionary War on Wednesday*

*A*ll through early childhood, my brothers and I collected small green army soldiers to play with. We pretended they had battles and went on secret missions. One of my army men was different from all the rest: a tiny gold statue that had a name engraved at the bottom, *General Omar Bradley.* Back then, I didn't know who Omar Bradley was, except that he was a general in World War II. He was my hero and commanded all my green army men with courage and kindness. Eventually, he disappeared during one of our moves. I imagine he would seem very small to me now if I still had him. But in memory, the tiny gold general looms large and luminous.

Heroes—even imaginary ones— can inspire you to become a hero yourself.

Is Annie a treasure? Jack wondered. He'd always thought of a "treasure" as something super valuable, like gold or silver or rare jewels. But right now Annie seemed more valuable than any of those things. She seemed like the most valuable thing in the world.

—Blizzard of the Blue Moon

My older sister, Natalie, has always been my hero. In third grade, my teacher was strict and often unkind to kids. So every morning, walking from the bus to my classroom, I'd feel a pain in my stomach. When I told Natalie about my stomachaches, she offered to help. Natalie was in ninth grade in the same school. I admired everything about her—her smart thoughts, her funny jokes, the books she read, her handwriting, her appearance, her bedroom furniture. So I was honored when she began escorting me from the bus into the school every morning. At the door of my classroom, she'd give me a hug and wish me luck. With Natalie's help, over time, I started feeling stronger and more able to handle things. And all my stomach pains ended.

Always try to give comfort to a family member who's having a hard time.

"Help the bucket brigade!" Basho said to Jack and Annie. "Get water from the river!" . . .

Jack and Annie hurried down to the river. Jack filled their wooden bucket. With water inside, it was so heavy he couldn't lift it.

"Do it together!" said Annie.

"Right!" said Jack.

Using all their strength, Jack and Annie carried their bucket up the bank of the river. . . . Over and over, Jack and Annie hauled buckets of water back and forth from the river to the line of firefighters.

—Dragon of the Red Dawn

*E*very Thursday, there was a parade on the field at Fort Monroe. One day, the parade honored a boy for rescuing a two-year-old who'd fallen into a pond. I was so impressed by the celebration of that boy that for a while, whenever I was near water, I kept an eye out for a toddler to save. Fortunately, none crossed my path, as I didn't know how to swim.

But I *could* save my most precious possessions: my dolls. I wanted to be prepared in case of disaster. So I decided to have a fire drill with them.

Imagining our house was on fire, I threw all the dolls (there were many) out the window of my second-floor bedroom. I timed myself racing down the stairs and outdoors to retrieve them. As no dolls had been hurt in their fall, I was reassured I could quickly save them in case of fire.

Always be ready to assist others in case of a disaster. It helps to be prepared.

BE DARING,
BUT NOT FOOLISH

6

Leonardo was already staggering toward the edge of the steep hill with the flying machine on his back. It was so heavy that he could hardly stand up.

"Leonardo, stop!" cried Annie. "You need a motor!"

But Leonardo bent his legs and lowered his body close to the ground. He grabbed the two large handles and pulled them toward his chest. The huge wings rose into the air.

"The Great Bird raises its wings and is pushed by the wind!" shouted Leonardo.

"Noooo!" yelled Jack and Annie.

—*Monday with a Mad Genius*

When I was in kindergarten in Fort Monroe, during Easter vacation, I decided to try to fly like a bird. I'd heard that people couldn't fly, but I needed to test that for myself. I invited my four-year-old brother, Michael, to accompany me, and we walked to a playground near our house. With Michael watching hopefully, I climbed to the top of the sliding board. Bending my legs and flapping my arms, I jumped—and landed hard in the dirt. The landing knocked the breath out of me, and I skinned my knees, but I wasn't seriously hurt. Then I brushed myself off, and Michael and I headed back home, finally accepting the truth that humans can't fly.

Search for answers to big questions. But try not to physically harm yourself in the process.

"Okay, so what's your point?" Jack said, slightly hurt. "That I'm not brave? I already know that."

"No, that you *are* brave, *really* brave," said Annie. "You did those things even though you were afraid. I was afraid, too. But to us, saving Cria and bringing her home to Topa was more important than our fears. So we crossed the bridge. We entered the city. And we walked Cria down the mountain trail."

"So, we were brave after all?" said Jack.

"Yes. People can't be brave unless they're first afraid," said Annie. "Being afraid and being brave totally go together."

—Late Lunch with Llamas

I had a lot of fears when I was a kid. Nightly, I checked under my covers for tarantulas, fire ants, and centipedes, to name a few scary things I've never encountered in my life.

I was most afraid, though, of the one thing I *did* encounter day and night: the ocean. For two years, we lived in a military house on a lonely outcropping of shore in Virginia Beach. Our windows were always damp with spray from waves crashing against the seawall.

My brothers enjoyed the water, but I feared everything about it: jellyfish; tangled, slimy strings of seaweed; and, of course, tidal waves.

Ashamed of my fear, one morning, I put on my bathing suit and a pair of sneakers. With no one else around, I crossed the sand and walked directly into the water. I didn't get far before a small wave knocked me down. Splashing wildly, I scrambled to stand up. It was hard to run in my waterlogged sneakers, but I ran back out of the ocean and all the way home.

From then on, I was okay with that fear, because I'd given the ocean a serious try. I happily resumed land activities such as sitting on top of a sand dune with my brother Michael, pretending we had our own dolphins and could ride out to sea.

Face your fear.
Then relax and do what
makes you happy.

"And Thomas Edison!" said Annie.

"Magic!" gasped Jack. "Thousands of years . . . you depend on fire for light . . . then one day . . . you flip a switch . . . *presto!* . . . a glass bulb lights up. . . ."

—Night of the New Magicians

Michael, Bill, and I would often interrupt our play with snack time back at home. Mom would serve us graham crackers and Kool-Aid in paper cups. One day, sitting on the porch steps, I squeezed my paper cup, making the Kool-Aid rise toward the top.

I was astonished! I'd invented a way to create more Kool-Aid! The boys couldn't have been more excited. I received lots of praise from them for my brilliant discovery.

I vaguely remember that later, someone (probably our sister Natalie) set us straight: there wasn't more Kool-Aid in the cup, even though it looked that way.

Be curious and creative, and maybe someday you really will *discover something new.*

FIND OUT WHO YOU ARE

7

"Actually, nothing was being mean," said Jack. "The army ants were just marching. That's what army ants do."

"The piranhas were just being piranhas," said Annie.

"The snake was just being a snake," said Jack.

"The crocodile was just being a crocodile," said Annie.

—Afternoon on the Amazon

nimals seem to know who they are and what they do. But humans, I think, can't begin to learn about themselves until they start exploring the world. I tried to do many things when I was growing up. To name just a few, I tried singing, swimming, tap dancing, ballet, archery, baton twirling, painting, cooking, sewing, playing baseball, waterskiing, horseback riding, tennis, ice-skating, running fast, and jumping high.

I wasn't good at *any* of these things. But I learned who I was: I was a person who tried things.

———

Be open to all kinds of possibilities. Sooner or later, you'll figure out who you're not— and who you are.

"A big day for baseball," said Annie.

"Yep, a really big day," said Jack. He kept reading:

"In 1947, Robinson was voted Rookie of the Year. And in 1955, he was a World Series champion."

"What's Rookie of the Year?" Annie asked.

"The best new player," said Jack. He read on:

"Jackie Robinson was not just a great baseball player. He also showed heroic strength in the face of racism. 'I'm not concerned with your liking or disliking me . . . ,' he once said. 'All I ask is that you respect me as a human being.' His talent and courage helped inspire the civil rights movement."

—A Big Day for Baseball

When I was six, twin girls my age moved in next door. I decided to go over and introduce myself.

I climbed the steps to their porch and knocked on the front door. The girls came outside, and for no reason, they started calling me names. They taunted me and pushed me off the porch. In spite of what they did, I climbed back up the steps. Again, they made fun of me and pushed me off the porch. This happened over and over, and each time, their name-calling grew worse.

Finally, I gave up trying to make friends with the twins. I headed home, carrying the burden of humiliation. On my way, I wished I'd left when they'd first acted mean. I wished I'd taken better care of myself. Why I didn't just walk away from those mean girls sooner has always been a mystery to me.

———

Don't put up with bullies.
Respect yourself. Walk away.

Exhausted, Jack lay back on his bed. He squeezed his eyes shut. He tried to remember the details of their adventures in Camelot and the Otherworld. . . .

Jack sat up. All at once, he felt very awake. He turned to a clean page in his notebook. He grabbed his pencil and wrote:

It all started when we saw the white dove in the twilight. . . .

Using his memory and his imagination, Jack kept writing, doing his part to keep the legend of King Arthur, the Knights of the Round Table, Merlin, and Morgan le Fay alive.

As the snow swirled outside his window, Jack wrote and wrote and wrote . . . *his* story of their Christmas in Camelot.

—Christmas in Camelot

When I was eight, I was given a rubber ball of many colors. It had nubby skin and a lively bounce. I named it All-Ball. Every day for weeks, I bounced All-Ball in our driveway and talked softly, making up stories. One day, a neighborhood dog grabbed All-Ball and tore it to pieces in front of my eyes. I became hysterical. I ran into the house, screaming, and threw myself on my bed, sobbing. My dad and brothers felt so bad for me, they picked up the scraps of All-Ball from the yard and brought them to me. For weeks afterward, I slept with those torn pieces under my pillow.

Why did I grieve so much for a ball? I don't really know, but I do know that every time I bounced All-Ball, the door to my imagination would swing open. As I shared stories with that ball, we became best friends. After I lost All-Ball, I learned that there were many ways to make up stories. I played more with kids from the neighborhood. There's a photo of me from that time in which I'm standing in front of some other kids with my hands on my hips, and I have a scary expression on my face. I must have been telling them a story. My dream eventually became to write stories for people to read. Oddly, a brightly colored bouncing ball might have started me down that path.

The loss of a favorite possession can be heartbreaking. But it might help you learn something important about yourself.

GIVE YOUR
GIFTS TO THE WORLD

8

"Morgan!" cried Annie.

She threw her arms around the enchantress. Jack jumped up and hugged Morgan, too. . . .

"Look," said Annie. She reached into Jack's pack and pulled out the piece of painted bark. "A gift from a kangaroo."

—Dingoes at Dinnertime

My brothers and I didn't get an allowance, so we never had any money. If our dad took us into a dime store, he'd usually give us a quarter to buy whatever we wanted, which was most often comic books. If we wanted something big, we waited for our birthdays or Christmas.

When Dad was in Korea, Mom's birthday was coming up, and we had no money to buy her a gift.

The day before her birthday, I was riding my bike past a new Planters Peanuts store that was having a grand opening in Daytona Beach, Florida, where we lived at that time. The store was giving away freebies! I raced home to the boys to share the good news. We hurried back to the store, where a clerk gave each of us a small tin peanut bowl. At the bottom of each bowl was Mr. Peanut in his top hat and white gloves.

Mom received three of those peanut bowls for her birthday, and she said they were some of the best gifts she'd ever been given.

Even if you don't have money,
try to find a way to give gifts
to your loved ones. They'll almost
certainly be grateful.

Jack opened his mouth to speak—but suddenly, *horribly,* he couldn't think of anything to say!

Holding the wand in midair, Jack turned to Annie. She looked confused, too. Their hour of being great stage magicians had ended. The magic was over.

Some people yelled from the audience. Jack felt embarrassed and self-conscious. He couldn't believe he was trying to perform magic in front of a gazillion people.

—Hurry Up, Houdini!

Growing up, I loved to sing and would sing a lot at home. I even thought I might have a career as a singer. I had an old songbook I would read from, making up my own tunes. I still remember words from one of the songs: "I'm Captain Jinks of the Horse Marines. I give my horse good corn and beans."

One day, years later, when the local community theater announced tryouts for the musical *Cinderella,* I was certain I was perfect for the part. For days, I practiced the audition song in my room: *"In my own little corner, in my own little chair, I can be whatever I want to be. . . ."* I memorized the words and, feeling fairly confident, went to the theater.

At the audition, everyone was smiling and friendly, which made me feel even more confident. But when I got onstage, a terrible thing happened. The piano player started playing the song. I'd never sung the song with musical accompaniment! I didn't know where to come in. I just stood there with my mouth open! The piano player started the song again and again. Each time, I just stood there with my mouth open, until finally, I hurried off the stage, horrified and embarrassed.

Fortunately, at a later date, I tried out for a play that wasn't a musical, and I got the part. I went on to act in many plays after that. I discovered I didn't have to sing to enjoy performing onstage. For the next few years, acting was the main way for me to share my gift with others.

Even if you fall on your face, don't be afraid to get up and reach for the stars again.

"Charles Dickens, Lady Augusta Gregory, Louis Armstrong, Wolfgang Amadeus Mozart, and all other great artists live on through their work," said Morgan.

"You put your four friends on the path to giving their gifts to the world," said Kathleen.

"And the world *still* receives their gifts," said Teddy.

"You accomplished your mission," Merlin said to Jack and Annie. "Thank you for helping bring happiness to millions."

—A Ghost Tale for Christmas Time

When my twin brother, Bill, and I were in third grade, our army post had a contest for outdoor Christmas decorations. Bill kept reminding our parents about the contest, until Mom finally told him she was too busy and if he wanted decorations, he should try making some himself.

So Bill got to work. He used his imagination and made a small handwritten sign on a piece of cardboard, then posted it in front of our house. The sign read:

Bill Pope says Merry Christmas

I'm afraid most people missed Bill's sign, as they were distracted by all the store-bought decorations and dazzling lights in the neighborhood. If they did miss it, I'm sorry. Bill's Christmas gift to the world was perfect.

*Share your own message
with the world. If you have a good
heart, you can't go wrong.*

FIND WAYS TO BRING

ORDER TO YOUR LIFE

9

A few people began staring at the strange small soldier with the high-pitched voice.

Jack couldn't take it anymore. He had to get Annie away before it was too late!

He shoved his notebook into his bag.

"I have to go!" he shouted to Plato.

The philosopher looked surprised.

Jack was afraid to tell him that Annie had broken the rules.

—*Hour of the Olympics*

*A*s we moved from house to house, I often shared a bedroom with my brothers. There were lots of advantages to that: After the lights went out, we could discuss our days. We could also talk to each other as soon as we woke up. And if we were really sharp, while still in our beds, we could make first dibs on TV shows. The boys and I invented rules for ourselves. If you were the first to "dib" a particular show, the matter was instantly settled. We all had to watch that show, whether we liked it or not.

We made rules about eating, too. Our favorite pie was lemon meringue. If you were the last one to finish, you'd be within your rights to hold out your last bite and try to arouse envy in the others. In fact, you were expected to wave your fork in the faces of the other two and say *"Mmm-mmm!"* The other two would never dare snatch the forbidden piece—that was a rule.

But one day, on an impulse, I *did* snatch the last bite off Bill's fork! We all screamed with delight because I'd shamelessly broken one of our rules! Bill, who'd just lost his last bite of pie, was laughing so hard he didn't even mind!

If it doesn't hurt anyone,
now and then you can break
a rule—especially if it's a
rule you've made up yourself.

Jack caught his breath as he looked around Leonardo's studio.

There were mirrors, wooden trunks, globes, paint pots, and brushes. Sketches, paintings, and handmade maps were all over the walls. There were stacks of old books, half-built furniture, piled-up papers, theater masks, pieces of costumes, and musical instruments.

"Oh, man," murmured Jack. "I *love* this room."

—Monday with a Mad Genius

When I was ten and we moved to the house on the ocean, I was given a small room of my own. My mother offered to fix it up and asked what color I'd like it to be. I looked at magazines and came across a yellow room I liked. So I said yellow. But I asked my mother to hold off preparing my new room until the day of my annual dental appointment. I thought if I had a beautiful room to return to, I'd have something to look forward to while having my teeth worked on.

The big day finally came. When I got home from the dentist, Mom led me upstairs, with my brothers trailing behind. We stood at the door of my room, and I saw a new yellow bedspread, yellow curtains, and a yellow rug. Most touching of all, sitting on my dresser was a ceramic figurine of two yellow birds perched on a branch.

The yellow room inspired me to keep my space extremely neat for a while. I tried to keep myself neat, too. I might have gone too far when I asked Mom to start ironing my pajamas.

———

Do what you can to make your corner of the world special and inviting.

"No!" Jack said. "We have to stay. We can't give up. That's on the list—*Don't give up.*"

Jack pulled out their list to show Clara Barton.

"Oh, yes," she said, nodding. "I see one of my nurses has written down the things I often say. Let me add one thing more—*Do not forget the ones who love you.*"

—*Civil War on Sunday*

*I*n my yellow room, I set about to organize my life. Of course, this involved writing a list of things to do after school. I found a copy of that list many years later. It was pretty straightforward.

Change clothes
Get exercise
Eat dinner
Do homework
Take a bath
Put lotion on hands
Say prayers
Go to sleep

Put lotion on hands? That strikes me now as a little odd. Maybe I'd just discovered that hand lotion existed.

The other odd thing I did was to invent a prayer I thought would cover every possible problem. I still remember it:

"God, protect us from animals, insects, intruders, prowlers, burglars, sickness, fire, death, and disease."

I seemed overly concerned about someone breaking into the house, as I listed three ways to describe it. But my prayers were answered: No one ever broke into our house. No animals or insects ever harmed any of us. And sickness, fire, death, and disease, at least in my early years, stayed away.

———

Take charge when possible.
Otherwise, ask for help.

HONOR YOUR LOVED ONES

10

"We're home," whispered Annie.

The woods were lit with a golden late-afternoon light. The sun was about to set.

No time had passed since they'd left Frog Creek.

"Ja-ack! An-nie!" a voice called from the distance.

"That's Mom," said Annie.

Jack saw their mother far away. She was standing in front of their house. She looked tiny.

"An-nie! Ja-ack!" she called.

—*Dinosaurs Before Dark*

Our mother was very Southern and very funny. She grew up on a peanut farm in Alabama and was teaching second grade when our dad, an army officer, married her. Overnight, Mom became a military wife and was whisked away to travel around the world and raise four children. She rose to every occasion, making an ordered and cozy home every year or two, wherever we landed. She kept us well fed and well clothed and found all kinds of free lessons to help us explore our talents. She gave us lots of freedom to be the eccentric kids we all were. Best of all, she encouraged the four of us to deeply care for one another.

I can't remember Mom ever punishing us. But she had great authority and would be very dramatic if we got to be too much, raising her arms to the sky and saying in an exaggerated Southern accent, "O Lord, why was I evah born?" Or "You children are the most horrible creatures evah put on the face of the earth!" We would laugh at her drama, and she would laugh, too. But we always stopped doing the thing she didn't want us to do.

There are many ways
to express annoyance
and frustration. Doing it
with a sense of humor
might be the best.

"So the fourth secret is *take care of someone who needs you*," said Annie. "I guess that could mean lots of things. Like take care of a sad person, a baby, a puppy, or a new kid in school. . . ."

Jack nodded. "Yep," he said. "And maybe it works the other way, too."

"What do you mean?" said Annie.

"I think sometimes you can make other people happy by letting *them* take care of *you*," Jack said.

"Oh, right," said Annie. "It seems to make Mom and Dad happy to take care of us. . . . We better hurry."

"Yep, let's go make Mom and Dad happy—" said Jack, laughing.

"By letting them take care of us!" said Annie.

—Eve of the Emperor Penguin

*E*ven though our army colonel dad had been a combat soldier in World War II, he was very tenderhearted. He adored small children and would do anything for us. When Bill and I had our fifth-birthday party, three-year-old Michael expected to be celebrated, too. So Dad hid behind some bushes near our house with a sack of presents, and as the guests arrived, he gave them each a wrapped gift to give to Michael.

Dad hid in the bushes another time. He'd been away from the family for a year, stationed in Korea. We missed him every day. I took his absence especially hard. I had insomnia and would often steal away alone to cry about his being gone.

On the day Dad was scheduled to return, we were incredibly excited. At school that day, I couldn't sit still. I couldn't stop smiling and telling others our dad was coming home.

That afternoon, the boys and I sped home on our bikes. We parked in the driveway and started for the house. Suddenly Dad jumped out from behind a bush! We screamed and laughed and threw our arms around him. I remember *he* cried. That time, too, he had a bag of presents. I still have a little carved wooden music box he brought back to me.

Don't take parents and caregivers for granted. Tell them you're grateful for all they do.

Jack saw their house in the distance.
It looked warm and cozy.

The porch light glowed. The moon shone overhead.

"Home," he whispered.

"Home," said Annie.

She started running. Jack took off after her, running to the place that they both loved the best.

—Polar Bears Past Bedtime

I was so attached to my family that I dreaded being separated from any of them. Just as I suffered when my dad went to Korea, I wept for days after my sister, Natalie, went off to college. When my brother Michael was in the hospital overnight, I went through a whole box of tissues. On the first day of third grade, when they tried to put my twin brother, Bill, in a different classroom from mine, I made such a scene that the principal let us stay together.

I've never forgotten this simple, searing memory: On a cloudy afternoon, I was riding my bike to our house on the ocean. Suddenly the sky grew black, and a hard rain started to fall. I imagined that all the family—Mom, Dad, Natalie, Bill, and Michael—would be worried about me. I stood up on my pedals and used all my strength to ride against the wet wind. I was desperate to get home and be with my family, warm, dry, and safe inside our house, out of the storm.

Hold on to the good memories of your loved ones. Those memories can comfort you all your life.

Note from the Author

When I was living in New York City in the early 1990s, Random House asked me to consider writing a chapter-book series for beginning readers. I wasn't sure that would be a good fit for me, as I was in the middle of several other projects for older readers. I asked my twin brother to meet me in Fort Monroe, where he and I had once been little kids ourselves, to help me decide what to do.

Bill picked me up at the airport in Norfolk, and we drove to the post. As we sat together again on the parade field, the bells from the Chapel of the Centurion started to ring. Everything looked and felt the same as it had decades earlier. I had an aching desire to be seven again and carry a cardboard box across the field and create more Kool-Aid by squeezing a paper cup.

By the time we left Fort Monroe, I'd decided to turn away from my other projects and commit to writing the series for new readers. It would be the best way, I thought, to slip back into the magical world of childhood and rediscover the joy of play and impossibility.

Jack laughed. Suddenly he felt very happy.

He couldn't explain what had happened today. But he knew for sure that their trip in the magic tree house had been real.

Absolutely real.

"Tomorrow," Jack said softly, "we'll go back to the woods."

—Dinosaurs Before Dark

The People and Places
From My Memories

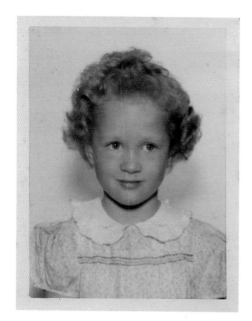

Me

Bill, my twin brother

Michael, my younger brother

Natalie, my older sister

Our dad and mom

Michael, me, and Bill—the Christmas when Bill made his sign

Me and my hero: my big sister, Natalie
(Salzburg, Austria)

Me, age three, driving my car. (My hair must have stopped traffic.)

Entrance to the area where we lived at Fort Monroe, surrounded by a moat

A beloved tree off the parade field. It always beckoned to be climbed.

Our house on the lonely Virginia shore

Our puppy, Bailey,
admiring Teddy

Kisses from Little Bear

MARY POPE OSBORNE

is the author of many novels, picture books, story collections, and nonfiction books. Her *New York Times* number one bestselling Magic Tree House® series has been translated into numerous languages around the world. Highly recommended by parents and educators everywhere, the series introduces young readers to different cultures and times in history, as well as to the world's legacy of ancient myth and storytelling. She is also the creator of the Magic Tree House Classroom Adventures Program. Mary and her husband, writer Will Osborne (co-creator of the Magic Tree House® Fact Tracker series and many Magic Tree House musicals), live in the Berkshires of Massachusetts with their two dogs, Wilson and Penny.